Skydiving

INSIDE STORY

Copyright © ticktock Entertainment Ltd 2006
First published in Great Britain in 2006 by ticktock Media Ltd,
Unit 2, Orchard Business Centre, North Farm Road,
Tunbridge Wells, Kent TN2 3XF

ISBN 1 86007 845 1

Printed in China

**The author would like to thank Mark Maynard
of adrenaline-adventures.co.uk for his help in the
writing of this book.**

Picture credits (t=top; b=bottom; c=centre; l=left; r=right):
3, 6B, 7T, 7BR, 11T, 12B, 13BR, 15, 18B, 19T, 21B Mark Maynard;
13T chris fotoman smith/Alamy; 26T Red Bull/DanielGrund.com; 26B,
27T Red Bull/flohagena.de; 27BRC Red Bull/Bernhard Spöttel.

Every effort has been made to trace the copyright holders, and we
apologise in advance for any unintentional omissions. We would be
pleased to insert the appropriate acknowledgements in any subsequent
edition of this publication.

Neither the publishers nor the author shall be liable for any bodily harm
or damage to property whatsoever that may be caused or sustained as
a result of conducting any of the activities featured in this book.

Contents

Introduction

Skydiving is parachuting with a plus.
The skydiver jumps from a plane
and falls for about **45** seconds
before opening the parachute.
The time in the air before the
parachute opens is called freefall.

NOT A ROLLERCOASTER

Most skydivers use rectangular parachutes, which
stay up longer and are easier to control than
circular ones. They usually jump from planes
flying at about 4000 metres (13,000 feet)
and can hit speeds of 190 kilometres per
hour (120mph) in freefall. That may sound
like a rollercoaster ride, but divers do not
have a strong sense of falling. They feel
as though they are floating on air.

MOVING WITH STYLE

Skydivers can spin and tumble, or glide
forward, back, left and right on the air flow.
That's what they mean when they say they feel
as free as a bird. As the ground gets closer, they
have to decide exactly when to open the 'chute.

Enjoying the jump
safely, that's what
this sport is all about.

SKYDIVING FACTS - DID YOU KNOW?

Parachutes were invented 200 years ago, but the sport
of skydiving only developed about 50 years ago. Now there
are over 5 million jumps a year, all around the world.

TANDEM

STATIC LINE JUMPS

SOLO

TEAM SKYDIVING

In a tandem skydive, the student is linked to an instructor for safety.

Linking up mid-air is a whole new set of skills to learn.

Skydiving Equipment

Safety is vital in skydiving. The right equipment must be used on every jump. Learning how to use the equipment correctly is an essential part of skydive training.

PARACHUTES

Skydivers always wear a main parachute, plus a back-up in case things go wrong. Learning how to pack a parachute is an essential part of skydive training.

JUMPSUITS

A jumpsuit is a one-piece costume that zips up at the front. Tight, smooth jumpsuits are best for moving quickly through the air.

HELMETS

Head protection must always be worn. This can be a hard hat, or a leather helmet.

GOGGLES

All skydivers protect their eyes during freefall. Some wear goggles, others use a helmet with a visor.

ALTIMETERS

Altimeters show skydivers how far they are from the ground. They look like big watches and are usually worn on the wrist or the back of the hand.

The large fabric part of the parachute is called the canopy.

SKYDIVING FACTS - DID YOU KNOW?

Reserve parachutes are opened and given a full safety check every 180 days, even if they have not been used. Reserve 'chutes save lives.

Hard hats or padded leather helmets are worn on every dive

TRUE STORIES

In 1792, France's Jacques Garnerin jumped from an air balloon at 90 metres (3000 feet) using one of the very first parachutes. He made a safe landing.

The straps of the parachute are fixed around the shoulders, waist and legs.

Sound altimeters beep when it's time to open the 'chute for a safe landing.

The main and reserve parachutes are kept in a skydive backpack.

First Flight

The thrill starts as the student walks out across the airfield for the first skydiving flight. This is it... the adventure begins.

IN THE PLANE

Imagine your first flight as a skydiver. The plane circles as it climbs high above the airfield. The safety checks have been done and you are linked with your instructor who will control the flight. The plane doors open and you feel a blast of cold air. Your heart is pumping and your mouth is dry. You wait for the signal to jump... then you go!

Jumping out of the plane is scary, but skydivers know they have the courage to do it.

FREEFALL

As the plane soars away, you are in freefall. You feel the rush of air on your body. The instructor pulls the ripcord to open the parachute. You feel a tug as the canopy opens to bring you slowly to earth. You land safely thanks to what you learned in training. Like most students, you can't wait to do it all again.

For the first jump, the student is harnessed to an instructor who controls the parachute.

SKYDIVING FACTS - DID YOU KNOW?

US Army Captain Albert Berry made the first parachute jump from a moving aeroplane over Missouri, US, on March 1, 1912.

Medium weight black leather gloves with a velcro closure.

TRUE STORIES

Being called a skygod sounds good, but it's not. It's a nickname for skydivers with big egos who think they know it all. Good skydivers know there is always something new to learn.

An electronic 'audible' logs information for up to 200 jumps.

Weight vests are sometimes worn by lightweight skydivers to provide stability.

It Takes Two

For most people, their first jump is a tandem jump with an instructor. A special harness attaches the student to the instructor, who carries the parachute. Tandem jumps are good for beginners because the instructor decides when to open the parachute. The student can just enjoy the experience.

FLYING HIGH

For a tandem flight, the plane goes up to around 3650 metres (12,000 feet), the height for most skydives. Freefall lasts about 45 seconds. The instructor and student reach speeds of up to 190 kph (120 mph). At about 1500 metres (5000 feet) above the ground the instructor pulls the ripcord. A tiny 'pilot chute' pulls the parachute from the backpack, then the main 'chute opens.

IN-FLIGHT TRAINING

When the parachute opens, it slows down the speed of descent. The instructor shows the student how to control the parachute. This is done using the rigging lines, the fine cords attached to the parachute. The instructor takes control again at about 150 metres (500 feet) above the ground to make sure the flight ends with a good landing.

A student's first skydive. In a tandem flight, the student is in front with the instructor behind.

SKYDIVING FACTS - DID YOU KNOW?

Skydiving schools set a top weight limit of around 100kg (15 stone) for new skydivers wanting to try a tandem flight. The risk of injury is too great if you weigh more than this.

The stitching on a parachute is usually done with a sewing machine.

During the skydive the instructor makes sure the student is in the right position.

TRUE STORIES

California 2001. Camera woman Janice Davis had made more than 2000 jumps, but on her last skydive, by incredible bad luck, both her parachutes failed to open. Janice fell to her death.

After use, a parachute is checked and packed away.

If it is looked after properly, a parachute can last for many years.

On the Line

Static line jumps give skydivers an early taste of going solo. There is no instructor on this jump, but students do get help. A line links their parachute to a strong point inside the plane. When the skydiver jumps, the line from the plane pulls the parachute open.

SOLO FOR THE FIRST TIME

Static line jumps are made at about 900 metres (3000 feet) above the ground. The skydiver falls about 90 metres (300 feet) in 2-3 seconds. This is probably the most scary part of the jump. Then the link to the plane pulls open the 'chute and the student can enjoy the ride back down to earth.

TRAINING COMES FIRST

Students need around six hours of coaching before making their first static line jump. They learn how to exit the plane safely, guide their parachute and make a safe landing.

After opening the parachute, it takes about three minutes for the skydiver to reach the ground.

The static line is fastened securely inside the plane and opens the parachute automatically.

SKYDIVING FACTS - DID YOU KNOW?

Students making a first-time static line jump are usually in radio contact with instructors on the ground, who talk to them as they come down to land.

An instructor demonstrates the proper position for freefall.

TRUE STORIES

Canada 1994. Experienced solo skydiver Sharon McClelland fell 300 metres (10,000 feet) when her parachutes failed to open. Luckily, she landed in a muddy marsh... got up and walked away!

Three students learn how to guide their parachutes and land safely.

An instructor explains how to make a safe exit from the plane.

Out on Your Own

Skydivers want to go solo as soon as possible. They train hard for their first solo jump. There are many important things to learn, including how to lie during freefall, when to open the parachute, how to steer it, and what to do in an emergency. Training usually includes tandem jumps.

Every jump is different, even for experienced skydivers.

MOVING ON

Students usually learn to skydive through an official training course such as AFF (Accelerated Freefall). The AFF course is a series of eight jumps. Students must pass each stage before they can move on, so they make each jump several times to master the skill. Earning the right to go solo takes most students a total of 18 jumps.

SAFETY FIRST

In the USA, skydivers make three million jumps every year. About 30 a year die in accidents. Most of those are deaths not due to bad equipment; they are caused by human error and daredevil stunts that go wrong.

An instructor with a camera makes a record of a solo flight.

SKYDIVING FACTS – **DID YOU KNOW?**

New skydivers might think it would be a good idea to wear boots for their first jump, but they are wrong. Trainers with a flat sole are best.

A log book records conditions during the jump and how well the student did.

TRUE STORIES

Bangkok, 2004. 672 skydivers from 42 countries fell from the sky for the Queen of Thailand's birthday. Why 672? Six is a lucky number in Thailand. The Queen was 72.

The instructor will note areas that need improvement.

The log book gives a student the chance to look back and note progress.

Down to Earth

Skydivers aim for drop zones, areas kept clear for landings. The ground is marked so the drop zone can be seen from the air. Skydivers learn how to steer their parachutes by pulling on the cords that attach it to the harness.

EASY DOES IT

The drop zone is a large open area of a field or airfield kept clear of planes and vehicles for safety. Skydivers must make sure they steer away from any other skydiver coming in to land at the same time. In the final part of the descent, the skydiver pulls on two small cords. These act like brakes to help with a smooth landing.

ON THE SPOT

Experienced skydivers become very good at steering their parachutes. To test their landing skills, they jump from 300 metres (3000 feet) and open the parachute at once. Then they steer towards a tiny disc just 5cm (2 inches) in diameter. The disc is marked out in the Drop Zone and records hits electronically. The best skydivers hit the spot every time.

Skydivers start looking for the drop zone from about 300 metres (1000 feet) up.

Today's parachutes are light and easy to steer.

SKYDIVING FACTS - DID YOU KNOW?

Skydivers heading for the drop zone slow their descent by making smooth, wide turns with their parachutes. They steer into the wind for the best control.

Skydivers must be physically fit and mentally prepared for their jump

TRUE STORIES

Canada 2002. Mathieu Gagnon was sucked up into a thunder cloud during a storm. He was not badly hurt, but most skydivers would not have been so lucky. Skydivers don't go up when a storm is forecast.

Exiting the plane well is the first step to a good landing.

A safe landing. Time to reflect on how well the dive went and plan for the next one.

Team Skydiving

Solo skydiving is a thrill. But jumping as part of a skydiving team takes things to a whole new level. If one person on the team loses control, the rest will be in danger too. The best team players react quickly to what others are doing.

Team skydivers wear helmets with face guards to protect them from bumps and kicks.

FORMATION SKYDIVING

Formation skydiving teams show their skills in freefall. Teams are made up of 4, 8 or 16 skydivers. They work together to make shapes, like circles and diamonds, in the sky.

CANOPY FORMATION TEAMS.

Canopy is another word for the fabric part of a parachute. Canopy stacking teams make shapes in the air by steering together and linking their 'chutes after they have opened. They need a lot of skill to make sure the parachutes do not become tangled.

DISPLAY TEAMS

Fairs, carnivals, parties and sports teams hire display teams to celebrate their event. Skydivers leave trails of white, blue and red smoke as they speed through the air. During night skydives, they use flares to light the dark sky.

Skilled skydivers link up in mid-air to form shapes.

SKYDIVING FACTS - DID YOU KNOW?

When skydiving teams form a circle in the air, they call it "building a round".

144 skydivers link up in a square.

TRUE STORIES

There is a display team in Ohio called 'The E Team'. Members dress up as Elvis Presley for their skydives.

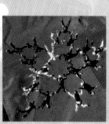

A pentagon (five skydivers) is the base shape of this link.

50 skydivers open their canopies and form a diamond.

Out There

Skydiving is always developing, because people want to try new things. Most skydivers fall face-down during freefall because it is the easiest position to control. But freefly skydivers may go head first, feet first, or even sitting down.

FREEFLY DIVING

Freefly teams make 3-D shapes in the air, as they twist and spin at speeds of up to 290 kph (180 mph). It's like watching top gym stars working out in the sky.

SURFING IN THE SKY

You don't need the ocean to go surfing. Skysurfs are when skydivers take their boards into the sky and surf across the air waves. They do loops, rolls and upside-down spins on their boards.

FLY LIKE A BIRD

Birdman suits are made by adding extra cloth between the arms, body and legs of a jumpsuit, allowing divers to glide through the air like a bird. The suit slows descent and doubles the time a skydiver has in freefall.

Surfers might think riding a wave is a thrill – but skydivers ride the air!

A birdman suit doubles the time the diver spends in freefall.

A birdman suit is a specially modified jumpsuit.

SKYDIVING FACTS - DID YOU KNOW?

Most of us think of 'chicken soup' as something we have for lunch, but in the skydiving world that's what they call a mid-air move that goes wrong.

TRUE STORIES

Nottinghamshire, 2004. Skydiving team the 'Brit Chicks' set a new world record when the 60 women all linked up in the sky at the same time.

Extra cloth between the arms.

Extra cloth between the legs.

The diver can swoop and glide mid-air, just like a bird.

Sky High

Skydiving from the edge of space is a dream many skydivers around the world are chasing. One plan is to jump from an air balloon 40,000 metres (130,000 feet) up in the sky. The skydiver would carry oxygen supplies, wear a space suit and travel at speeds up to 1450 kph (900 mph), faster than the speed of sound.

Scientific balloons like this one can rise to 40 km (26 miles) above the earth.

LONGEST FREEFALL

Captain Joe Kittinger of the U.S. Air Force set the record for the longest-ever skydive back in 1960. He was in freefall for 4 mins 36 secs. It took two parachutes to slow him down, but he landed safely. The jump took 13 mins 45 secs.

RECORD BREAKER

Captain Joe broke two more records that day. He made the highest ever jump from a balloon, at 31,333 metres (102,800 feet) above New Mexico. On his way down he hit a top speed of 988 kph (614 mph), making him the fastest human being of all time.

Joe Kittinger's record-breaking skydives are still an inspiration today.

SKYDIVING FACTS - DID YOU KNOW?

Future space skydivers will need 3-layer spacesuits to keep out the freezing cold. At 40,000 metres (130,000 feet) it is -112°F. (-80°C).

A balloon that travels to the edge of space needs to be big.

TRUE STORIES

The record for speed diving is held Michael Brooke from France.
In 1999 he jumped from a plane at the usual 4000 metres (13,000 feet) but accelerated in a head first position. Michael came down at over 520 kph (325 mph).

It must be strong and lightweight, and able to withstand the freezing cold.

It may take six hours to travel high enough in a balloon to set the record.

Record Breakers

Skydiving has many brave record breakers, such as Don Kellner of the USA. He holds the world record for the most skydives ever, with over 35,000. Here are some other skydiving heroes.

The utmost precision is needed for skydivers to link up mid-air.

TOP TEAM

Most skydiving teams are made up of 4, 8 or 16 people. But the world record for the most skydivers linking up in the sky at one time is an amazing 357. It took place in Thailand in 2004. Five big planes dropped the jumpers in a tight area from 6000 metres (20,000 feet). They all linked up for six seconds to set the record.

MOST SKYDIVES

Cheryl Stearns of the U.S.A. has made over 16,000 skydives. She holds the record for most skydives in a day. Cheryl did 352 skydives in 24 hours!

Cheryl Stearns is the world's most experienced woman skydiver.

SKYDIVING FACTS - DID YOU KNOW?

When skydivers meet to enjoy some fun jumps they call it a boogie. 'The World's Largest Boogie' is held every year in Rantoul, Illinois USA, when 6000 people join the party!

Skysurfers and sky skateboarders developed a new form of skydiving.

TRUE STORIES

In 1998, Herb Tanner from Ohio, USA became the world's oldest solo skydiver when he jumped into the record books at the age of 92.

Now professional skydivers jump with a variety of objects.

Camera crews record the jump for adverts or stunts in films.

Don't Try This At Home

BASE jumping began in the 1970s, but it has little to do with official skydiving. Jumpers leaps from high buildings, cliffs and bridges instead of a plane. They wear a parachute, but only have seconds to open it. BASE jumping is banned in much of the world, because there have been so many deaths.

SKY HIGH IN CHINA

China allows BASE jumping. In 2004, BASE jumpers from around the world came to Shanghai to leap off the Jin Mao Tower, the highest building in China at 420 metres (1378 feet). The day was well run and nobody was hurt.

BRIDGE DAY

Bridge Day is the biggest legal BASE jumping event in the world. It is held every year near Fayetteville in West Virginia, U.S.A. Up to 250,000 people watch 450 BASE jumpers going off a bridge 267 metres (876 feet) high. Jumpers must register, and they can only take part if they have completed 50 skydives or BASE jumps.

Finding a safe place to land can be tricky in a city. BASE jumpers must plan their landings carefully.

Cave jumpers launch into deep darkness.

SKYDIVING FACTS - DID YOU KNOW?

Unlike skydivers, most BASE jumpers do not carry a back-up parachute for when things go wrong. There isn't time to open it.

BASE is an acronym for the places that are jumped from:

TRUE STORIES

In 1912, stuntman Frederick Law jumped from the torch of the Statue of Liberty in New York. He was paid by a movie company. His death-defying feat may have been the first **BASE** jump.

Building.

Antenna, such as a mast.

Span, such as a bridge.

Earth, such as a cliff.

Around the World

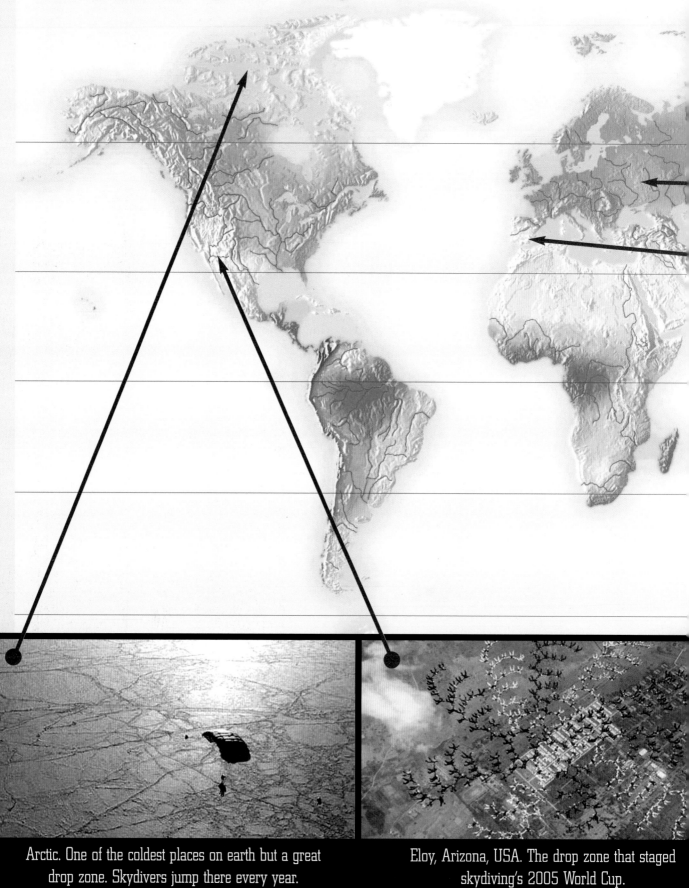

Arctic. One of the coldest places on earth but a great drop zone. Skydivers jump there every year.

Eloy, Arizona, USA. The drop zone that staged skydiving's 2005 World Cup.

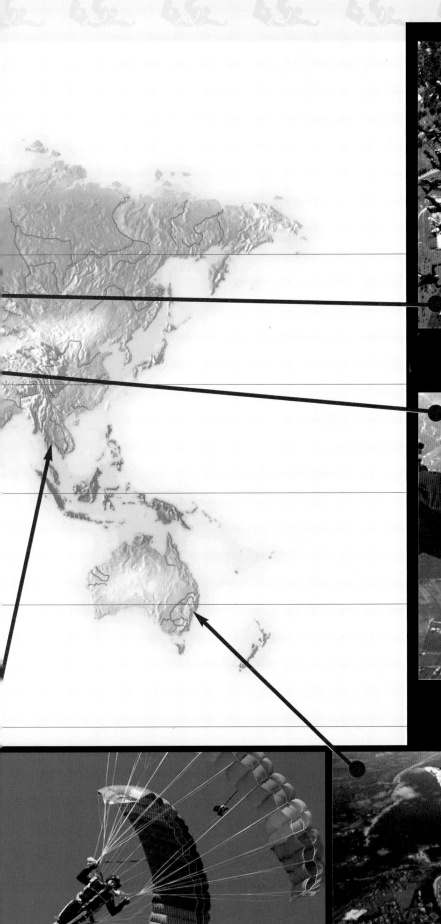

Stupino, Russia. Has hosted the European Championships.

Granada, Spain. A skydiving World Championships venue.

Bangkok, Thailand. 672 skydivers freefalled to celebrate the Queen's birthday in 2004.

Sydney, Australia. Another top location for the Skydiving World Championships.

Glossary

Altimeter
A piece of equipment that measures altitude.

Altitude
The height of an object above ground level.

BASE jumping
Making parachute jumps from buildings, bridges, cliffs and other tall structures. The name is taken from the first letters of the words Building, Antenna, Span and Earth.

Birdman suit
A special suit with extra fabric between the legs and sleeves, designed to catch air and slow the rate of descent to earth.

Canopy
Another name for the fabric part of a parachute.

'Chute
A short version of the word parachute.

Deploy
Open a parachute or a reserve chute.

Descent
The journey from high in the air to the ground.

Drop zone
An area of a field or airfield that is set aside and kept clear for parachutists to make safe landings.

Flare
A stage near the end of a descent where the jumper pulls on two cords that act like brakes and slow down the parachute.

Formation
A pattern made in the air by freefall jumpers linking hands and arms, or by skydivers linking their parachutes after opening them.

Freefall
The time that passes between jumping from a plane or balloon and pulling the ripcord to open the parachute.

reefly

ame for unusual positions taken by skydivers take
uring freefall, such as going head-first, feet first or
tting down.

Reserve 'chute

 smaller, emergency parachute that is carried by
 skydiver, and can be used if the main 'chute fails
 open.

Rigging

he lines that join the parachute to the riser straps
hich are linked to the harness worn by the skydiver.

ipcord

 special cord that is pulled to open the parachute.

isers

trong straps that link the skydiver's harness to the
gging of the parachute.

Skysurfing

Using a surfboard to perform tricks in the sky
during freefall.

Solo jump

A jump made by a single skydiver without
an instructor.

Static line

A line attached to a plane that is used to open a
parachute automatically after the skydiver has jumped.

Tandem

A type of jump made by a student, or sometimes an
older person. They are attached to an instructor who
operates the parachute.

Toggles

Small devices that gather the rigging lines of the
parachute. Pulling on the toggles allows the parachutist
to control the parachute.

Index